Weather Update

Climates

by Theresa Jarosz Alberti

Consultant:
Joseph M. Moran, PhD
Associate Director, Education Program
American Meteorological Society, Washington, D.C.

Capstone press

Mankato, Minnesota

Bridgestone Books are published by Capstone Press,
151 Good Counsel Drive, P.O. Box 669, Mankato, Minnesota 56002.
www.capstonepress.com

Library of Congress Cataloging-in-Publication Data
Alberti, Theresa Jarosz.
    Climates / by Theresa Jarosz Alberti.
        p. cm.—(Bridgestone books. Weather update)
    Includes bibliographical references and index.
    ISBN 0-7368-3735-3 (hardcover)
    1. Climatology—Juvenile literature. I. Title. II. Series.
QC981.3.A53 2005
551.6—dc22   2004010840

Summary: Introduces the main climates on earth, including tropical, temperate, polar,
    and dry climates.

Editorial Credits
Christopher Harbo, editor; Molly Nei, set designer; Maps.com, illustrator;
    Wanda Winch, photo researcher; Scott Thoms, photo editor

Photo Credits
Bruce Coleman Inc./Bob & Clara Calhoun, 20
Color-Pic Inc./Earl R. Degginger, 14
Corbis/Diego Lezama Orezzoli, 6; John Conrad, 12
Corel, 1
Dan Delaney Photography, cover (child), back cover
DigitalVision, 10, 16; Gerry Ellis and Michael Durham, 8
Getty Images Inc./David Noton, cover (background)
Photodisc/Jeremy Woodhouse, 18

Table of Contents

World Climates

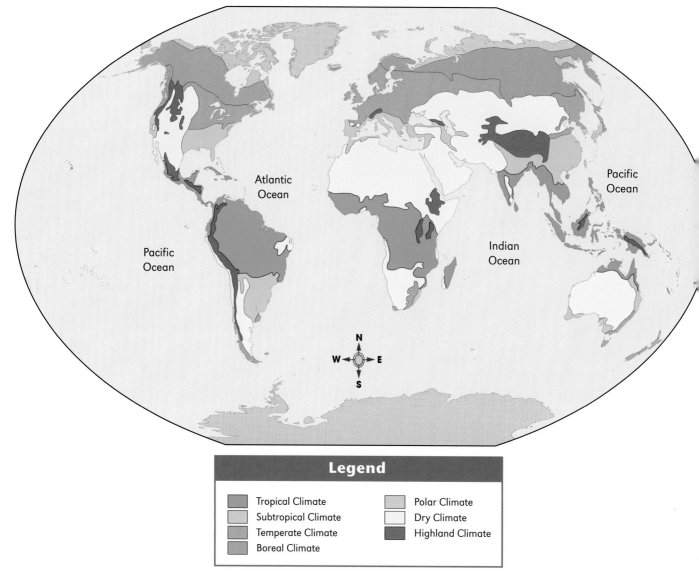

Atlantic Ocean

Pacific Ocean

Pacific Ocean

Indian Ocean

N
W E
S

Legend
Tropical Climate	Polar Climate
Subtropical Climate	Dry Climate
Temperate Climate	Highland Climate
Boreal Climate	

What Is Climate?

What is the weather like where you live? Climate is the **average** weather for an area over a long period of time. Temperature, wind, rain, and snow are all part of climate.

Earth has a variety of climate types. The main climate areas are tropical, temperate, polar, and dry. Earth also has some smaller climate areas. A warm, wet subtropical climate covers the southeastern United States. Cold **boreal** climates are found near polar areas. Highland climates have several climate areas at different heights on a mountain.

◄ Climate maps show the different climates around the world.

Tropical Climate

Tropical climates are hot and rainy. Temperatures usually stay above 70 degrees Fahrenheit (21 degrees Celsius) all year long. The heat and rain make the air **humid**. Humid air feels wet and sticky.

Tropical climates are found near the **equator**. The equator is an imaginary line around earth's middle. The main areas that have tropical climates are in Brazil, central Africa, Indonesia, and parts of Australia.

◀ Water pours over a waterfall in the lush, green forest of a tropical climate.

Life in a Tropical Climate

Heat and rain make tropical climates good places for plants to grow. **Rain forests** cover most of the land in a tropical climate. Rain forests receive at least 100 inches (254 centimeters) of rain each year. Vines, ferns, flowers, and mosses grow among thick forests of trees.

Tropical climates make good homes for many animals. Monkeys swing through the trees. Frogs, lizards, and snakes live in the brush. More kinds of birds live in rain forests than anywhere else.

◄ Two tree frogs cling to a branch in a rain forest.

Temperate Climate

The weather in a temperate climate changes during seasons. Winter, spring, summer, and autumn all have different weather patterns.

Temperate climates can be warm or cold. Warm temperate climates have rainy, cool winters. In cold temperate climates, snow falls in winter. Summers in both are warm and rainy.

Temperate climates are found in North America, Europe, and parts of Australia and Asia. These areas can have 20 to 60 inches (51 to 152 centimeters) of rain and snow each year.

◀ Some trees in temperate climates turn brilliant red, orange, and yellow colors in autumn.

Life in a Temperate Climate

Animals in temperate climates **adapt** to the changing seasons. Moose, wolves, and squirrels grow thicker fur in winter. Bears and skunks sleep through the cold winter months.

Many plants grow in temperate climates. Birch, maple, and pine trees live through warm and cold seasons. Some trees drop their leaves in autumn. They grow new leaves in spring. Many plants stop growing during winter. They bloom again in spring.

◀ A timber wolf stays warm with a thick winter coat of fur.

Polar Climate

Polar climates are the coldest places on earth. Most polar areas are always covered by snow and ice. The windy air is dry. Very little new snow falls each year. In the warmer areas, temperatures rise above freezing only two to four months of the year.

Antarctica, Greenland, northern Canada, and northern Siberia have polar climates. On July 21, 1983, Antarctica had the coldest temperature ever recorded. The temperature dropped to minus 129 degrees Fahrenheit (minus 89 degrees Celsius).

◀ Snow and jagged chunks of ice cover large areas in a polar climate.

Life in a Polar Climate

Animals in cold polar climates have ways to keep warm. Some animals dig **burrows** under the snow for shelter. Polar bears and musk oxen have thick layers of fat and fur. Downy feathers and fat protect penguins from the cold.

Some polar areas get warm enough to have a short growing season each year. Mosses and grasses can grow on polar land when the weather is mild. No plants grow in the coldest polar climates.

◄ A group of penguins waddles across the polar ice.

Dry Climate

Most dry climates have hot, windy desert lands. Deserts receive very little rainfall. Fewer than 10 inches (25 centimeters) fall each year. The daytime temperature is often hotter than 100 degrees Fahrenheit (38 degrees Celsius). Temperatures are very cold at night. Sand **dunes** and cloudless skies are common in many deserts.

Deserts are found in the dry climates of Africa, Australia, and Asia. North and South America also have desert lands.

◀ Huge sand dunes form in the Namib Desert in Africa.

Life in a Dry Climate

Animals in dry climates live with little water and high temperatures. Kangaroo rats don't drink water. They get water from the seeds they eat. Bats, snakes, and foxes sleep during the hot day and hunt during the cool night.

Desert plants have ways of living with little water, too. Cactus plants store water in their stems. The creosote bush can live up to two years without water.

What is the climate where you live? Compare the average weather of your area to earth's main climates.

◀ A kangaroo rat chews on a seed. The tiny rat gets all the water it needs from the seeds it eats.

Glossary

adapt (uh-DAPT)—to change to fit into an environment

average (AV-uh-rij)—a common amount of something; an average amount is found by adding figures together and dividing by the number of figures.

boreal (BOR-ee-uhl)—a climate area with very long, cold winters and short, cool summers

burrow (BUR-oh)—a hole in the ground in which an animal lives

dune (DOON)—a sand hill made by the wind

equator (i-KWAY-tur)—an imaginary line around the middle of earth; areas near the equator are usually warm and wet.

humid (HYOO-mid)—wet; humid air holds a lot of water vapor.

rain forest (RAYN FOR-ist)—a forest of tall trees that grows where the weather is rainy all year

Read More

Conrad, David. *The Weather Watcher.* Spyglass Books. Minneapolis: Compass Point Books, 2002.

O'Hare, Ted. *Studying Weather.* Weather Report. Vero Beach, Fla.: Rourke, 2003.

Internet Sites

FactHound offers a safe, fun way to find Internet sites related to this book. All of the sites on FactHound have been researched by our staff.

Here's how:
1. Visit *www.facthound.com*
2. Type in this special code **0736837353** for age-appropriate sites. Or enter a search word related to this book for a more general search.
3. Click on the **Fetch It** button.

FactHound will fetch the best sites for you!

Index